The
Connell Guide
to

The American Civil Rights Movement

by Stephen Tuck and Imaobong Umoren

Contents

NOTES

Introduction

May 3, 1963, Birmingham, Alabama. A police dog leaps up at a black high school student (see picture opposite). The boy stands defenceless, as a white policeman, eyes masked by mirrored glasses, grips his shirt. The *New York Times*, one of many newspapers to publish the picture on its front page, thundered: "the use of police dogs… to subdue schoolchildren in Birmingham is a national disgrace". The photograph of the scene quickly became one of the most iconic images of the civil rights movement.

This was day two of the so-called "Children's Crusade" in Birmingham, part of a summer of demonstrations championed by the Rev. Martin Luther King Jr. that sought to force the government to outlaw racial segregation. King reckoned Birmingham was "the most thoroughly segregated city in the United States". For many African Americans, the city had come to be known as Bombingham, on account of the dozens of home-made bombs set off at the homes of those who challenged the colour-line.

Birmingham was also a stronghold of the Ku Klux Klan. A few years before the Children's Crusade, a group of drunk white men had randomly grabbed a black man and castrated him. Local white business leaders might not endorse such violence, but they did support the Southern way of segregation in all areas of life, which led to African

Americans having to attend vastly inferior schools, being restricted to the back of public transport, and not being allowed to eat at department store lunch counters at all. Birmingham's notorious Commissioner of Public Safety (an ironic job title if ever there was one), Eugene "Bull" Connor, had vowed: "I may not be able to preserve segregation, but I'll die trying."

On day one of the Children's Crusade, thousands of high school students had marched on the streets and many hundreds ended up in jail. Faced by a second day of the crusade, and with no space left in the jails, Connor felt trapped. One officer remembered: "You could see Bull moving, looking, concerned, fidgety. He was just desperate. 'What the hell do I do?'" What he did was send in policemen with dogs, and authorize firemen to aim water hoses at the children, with jets of water strong enough to rip bark off trees. President John F. Kennedy was outraged. He told his brother Bobby, the Attorney General, "to get the people off the streets and the situation under control". Two months later, the President sent a civil rights bill to Congress to end segregation – the first major civil rights legislation since the Civil War era.

The photograph reflects the way that the civil rights movement is often remembered and celebrated. Here was a noble, youthful, non-violent protest that exposed the brutality and horrors of racial segregation in the American South. Here was a triumphant civil rights movement that shook the nation and prompted a president to act. Birmingham showed the power of media, and the power of the civil rights movement's strategy of set-piece confrontations. And Birmingham is a reminder of the importance of Martin Luther King. Later that summer, on August 28 1963, some quarter of a million people marched on Washington DC, where King delivered his famous "I have a dream" speech that inspires still.

Yet the photograph is also misleading. The teenager in the picture, Walter Gadsden, was not involved in the Children's Crusade. He was just crossing the street. Far from bending into a non-violent posture, Gadsden had raised his knee to knock back the dog – rumours spread in the black community that he broke the dog's jaw. The policeman, Dick Middleton, did not fit the caricature of a violent racist Southern sheriff. Middleton was reserved and had a good reputation. He kept his German Shepherd, Leo, on the leash. Just outside the frame of the photograph was a crowd, not of non-violent African American students but of adults who retaliated to police violence by throwing taunts, punches and bottles. In other words, the street scene on that May day was a far more complex, and far more interesting, human story than might appear at first sight.

So too was the Birmingham campaign. Though designed to put pressure on the federal government to outlaw segregation, the summer campaign was also part of a much longer, local story of simmering tensions about law enforcement and jobs. Birmingham was a city in rapid industrial decline. The local leader was the Rev. Fred Shuttlesworth, a champion of the poor. Though he invited King to come to Birmingham to attract media attention, the two pastors fell out when Shuttlesworth – who had been hospitalized by a fire hose jet – learned that King was willing to make a truce with city leaders in return for the desegregation of downtown lunch counters. "You may be Mr. Big now," Shuttlesworth warned, "but if you call it off, you'll be 'Mister Shit'."

In fact, King's campaign had already begun to

falter. His team had turned to children because ever fewer adults were willing to march. Some could not afford to go to prison or risk losing their jobs. Many did not share King's commitment to non-violence, and fought back. The famous Black Nationalist leader, Malcolm X, claimed: "The Negroes in Birmingham began to stab the crackers in the back and bust them up 'side their head – yes, they did. That's when Kennedy... said he was going to put out a civil rights bill." Nor did Kennedy's decision to introduce national civil rights legislation end the battle in Birmingham. Later that year, a bomb at one of the city's black Baptist churches killed four young girls at Sunday School.

The Birmingham campaign was part of a movement that went beyond the American South, and was not just about segregation. In the same year, 1963, there were hundreds of protests in the North and West of the United States about education and housing, employment and policing. There were protests against racism in other parts of the world, too – at the same time as the Birmingham Children's Crusade, there was a boycott of buses in Bristol, England, in protest at the colour bar in employment there. Little surprise, then, that the news – and photographs – about Birmingham were broadcast across the globe. Ahead of a conference of African leaders in Ethiopia, Prime Minister Milton Obote of Uganda sent an open letter to President Kennedy, which condemned the "inhuman treatment" of "our own kith and kin".

Grappling with the dangers of the Cold War, Kennedy – who had hitherto shown little appetite to respond to the civil rights movement – felt compelled to intervene.

The story of Birmingham, then, points to the long roots of the civil rights struggle, the importance of local stories and international connections, and the variety of tactics, goals and leadership. The civil rights movement has an uplifting history, to be sure: the story of one of America's greatest revolutions. But it was far more than a series of set-piece protests against Southern segregation, led by a heroic minister, that moved the conscience of a nation and inevitably climaxed in victory. Little wonder that the civil rights movement has generated a vast and rich scholarship from researchers from many different countries. We hope that this book provides an entry point into these exciting debates.

Few historical topics are as directly relevant to today. As Barack Obama, America's first African American president, observed at the dedication of a memorial to Martin Luther King in 2011, "our work, Dr. King's work, is not yet complete". As we write this book, stories about police brutality against African Americans, the rise of Black Lives Matter, and the policies of a President who questioned Obama's nationality and ran against his legacy, have returned the issues of racism and rights to the forefront of public consciousness. So the book concludes by looking at the continuing struggle against racism, and the ways in which the civil rights movement has been remembered and, all too often, mis-remembered.

When did the civil rights movement start?

It all began in Montgomery on December 1st 1955. A tired black seamstress, Rosa Parks, was returning home from her job in a local department store. The bus was crowded and, a couple of stops after boarding, she was asked by the driver to give up her seat to a white man, and move to the back as the law required her to do. She refused. She was arrested and fined $10, plus $4 in court fees.

The result was a swift and extremely well organised boycott. On the day of Rosa Parks's court hearing, the city's black population began refusing, *en masse*, to ride on the city's buses. They continued to do so for an extraordinary 381 days until, finally, the Supreme Court ordered the city authorities to back down and end segregation on their buses. It was this protest, led by, among others, a young pastor called Martin Luther King – the first modern mass demonstration against segregation in the US – which launched the civil rights movement.

That, at any rate, is the myth. But while the Montgomery bus boycott is a convenient starting point for journalists and popular histories, and rightly celebrated, it is by no means the real starting point of civil rights protest, which dates back to an era long before the activism of Rosa Parks and Martin Luther King. In 1982, Vincent Harding, a former activist and a friend of King's, published a long, comprehensive history entitled *There Is A River*. Harding pointed out that racism, and resistance, predated America even becoming a nation. His self-declared "celebrative history of the freedom struggle" took the metaphor of a river to "convey its long, continuous movement... sometimes powerful, tumultuous and roiling with life".

Of some 12 million Africans shipped to the New World, perhaps two million died during the crossing. Of the survivors, up to half a million ended up as slaves in Britain's North American colonies – starting in Virginia, in 1619. The system of slavery was contested at every turn: in Africa, on the Atlantic crossing, and after arrival in the New World. When Haiti gained independence from the French Empire in 1804, it set an example that inspired slaves, and unnerved masters, elsewhere.

There were hundreds of small-scale challenges to slavery in the United States, and a handful of larger uprisings. After the northern states of the USA ended slavery by the early 19th century, the famous "Underground Railroad" provided help for runaways from the South. Harriet Tubman, herself a runaway slave from Maryland in 1849, helped some 300 slaves to escape from the slave South during the ensuing decade. (In 2016, the Secretary of the Treasury announced that a picture of Tubman would be on the front of the $20 bill.) Those who remained in slavery, the vast majority, tried to maintain a sense of community, family and religious life that insisted upon their humanity.

By the time of the outbreak of the American Civil War in 1861, the four million slaves in the Southern states were ready to seize freedom, and thousands of them escaped to the North. Some served in the Union Army as spies, many more helped with menial tasks. In 1863, President Abraham Lincoln responded to the patriotism of slaves and the struggles of his army by issuing the Emancipation Proclamation. Altogether, during the war, nearly 200,000 black men served in uniform. When it ended in 1865, the passage of the 13th Amendment abolished slavery for good.

There was no simple progression from emancipation to civil rights a century later, though. For a season life improved for many newly freed men and women as they reunited families, searched for better jobs, established schools and churches, voted (men only) and won political office. But by the end of the 19th century, Southern states had introduced the so-called Jim Crow system of racial segregation and disfranchisement that was backed up by violence*. More than 3,000 African

Americans were lynched, many tortured in their final moments, the recorded screams and even body parts of some victims put on sale to souvenir hunters. The Southern Jim Crow system was in step with rising racism across the northern states of America and throughout the European empires. In 1954, the historian Rayford Logan famously called this period the "nadir" for African Americans.

Resistance took different forms in different places. At the height of Jim Crow in the American South, public confrontation was nigh on impossible. The most prominent black leader, the Alabama educator Booker T. Washington, secured his position by urging black southerners to accept segregation and subordinate status in return for industrial jobs and an end to violence. Many sought to turn "segregation into congregation" – to quote historian Earl Lewis – building communities and institutions that would later propel the civil rights movement. During the so-called Great Migration in the early 20th century, hundreds of thousands of rural black southerners moved to southern cities, or out of the South altogether.

In northern states, activists were able to lead high-profile protests. At the turn of the century, the tireless journalist and suffragist Ida B. Wells campaigned against lynching. The National Association for the Advancement of Colored People, founded in 1909, took up the cause (or took it over, some say, sidelining Wells), and began to challenge Jim Crow through the courts. The largest membership protest movement was led by the flamboyant Jamaican Black Nationalist Marcus Garvey – who was based in Harlem in New York – and celebrated links between black Americans, the Caribbean and Africa in the years after World War One.

During the Depression of the 1930s, protest movements proliferated in the South as well as the North: sharecroppers' and communist-led unions, African brotherhood societies, housewives' leagues, religious sects and church-based organizations, veterans' groups – the list is lengthy. Protest continued during World War Two, with black workers demanding inclusion in the defence industry, and black soldiers demanding integration in the army. At the same time white supremacy lost some of its potency, as Hitler gave racism a bad

IDA B. WELLS

Born a slave in Mississippi in 1862, Ida Wells looked after her six younger siblings following the death of her parents from yellow fever and later became a teacher.

In 1884, she was travelling in the ladies' carriage in a train in Memphis. The conductor told her to give up her seat to a white man and move to the crowded "Jim Crow" car. Wells refused. When the conductor tried to drag her out, she bit him on the hand and wedged herself in her seat. With colleagues, the conductor dragged her into the Jim Crow car. Afterwards, Wells sued the train company.

Almost a decade later, three of

name. Then Indian nationalists overthrew British rule in 1948, while the Cold War against the Soviet Union – a country with a reputation for good race relations – put pressure on America to live up to its constitutional ideals.

In other words, the rise of a nationwide, globally linked, civil rights movement was hardly a surprise. The forces which led to it had been simmering for years, with the war, in particular, acting as a powerful catalyst for change.

So when mass civil rights protests broke out in the 1960s they built on the efforts and experience of previous generations. Take Fannie Lou Hamer, a rural Southern sharecropper whose family had long refused to bow to Jim Crow. A devout Christian farm worker, she had learned self-reliance from a mother who "believed deeply that black was

her friends, who ran a grocery story in Memphis, were lynched by a mob which supported a rival (white) businessman. Wells launched a high-profile campaign against lynching, writing and lecturing about it and travelling to Europe to win support.

In particular, she challenged the widespread assumption that black men were lynched for rape, arguing that in many cases rape was not even claimed by the mob – and that in some cases the interracial sex which led to rape charges was consensual.

Wells was among the first prominent activists to demand women's rights as well as black rights. She criticized the racism she encountered within the (white) women's suffrage movement, but she also showed herself quite prepared to criticize black male leaders who did not challenge Jim Crow – despite being marginalized as a result. ●

beautiful". As a young woman, in her job measuring the pickings of sharecroppers, Hamer added a weight to the crops to counter the owner's unfair pay. Then, in Mississippi in 1963, she rose to prominence with a much publicised speech chastising President Lyndon Johnson.

In "The Long Civil Rights Movement" (2005), the historian Jacquelyn Dowd Hall challenged the idea that the Montgomery bus boycott marked the beginning of a different kind of civil rights movement. It was nothing of the kind, she said – if there was a watershed it was in the years between the Depression and the end of World War Two. That was really when the movement started.

What were the protesters trying to achieve?

"Freedom Now"; "I am a Man"; "Jobs and Justice"; "First Class Citizenship"; "Decent Housing Now"; "Equal Opportunity and Human Dignity"; "Teach Whites to be Nice"; "In the Fight For Human Rights".

These are a small sample of slogans that appeared on posters and banners held up by protesters during the civil rights era. This was an expanded vision of what equality should be – not just an end to segregation, but the desire by black Americans to be recognized as fully human and fully free: free from the terror and violence of white supremacy, free to choose how to live, and free to choose where to live and work, even what to wear.

For some, this vision of freedom extended beyond the African American community. Martin Luther King wrote the phrase "To Redeem the Soul of America" on a window at his headquarters to remind his colleagues that they were fighting to transform the nation, not just to win new rights. Ella Baker, a one-time colleague of King and influential protest leader in her own right, took this even further. "We are not fighting for the freedom of the Negro alone, but for the freedom of the human spirit," she said. This was "a larger freedom that encompasses mankind".

The first historians of the movement assumed that civil rights leaders were primarily concerned with the end of segregation and the right to vote. More recently, scholars have questioned this, arguing that there was always a broader conception of freedom underpinning the campaign. We get a sense of this in the subtitle of Barbara Ransby's 2003 biography of Ella Baker – *A Radical Democratic Vision* – while Thomas Jackson's 2007 biography of Martin Luther King recognizes in its subtitle – *From Civil Rights to Human Rights* – that economic justice became central to King's concerns.

What is now clear is that there was no single civil rights agenda. Even at the height of the movement, which was united in opposition to Jim Crow segregation, activists had a variety of ultimate goals. Some simply challenged segregation and sought the right to vote. Others concentrated on housing rights and job opportunities. Then there were those who were invested in the system of segregation, such as business owners in segregated communities, and they tended to be more cautious. As in most social movements, a majority did not actively participate in civil rights protest at all, because of fear, apathy or the pressures of their everyday lives.

The outlook of activists changed over time, too, shaped by their experience of protest. King's vision of a beloved community developed into a critique of materialism and militarism. More generally, civil rights lost ground to Black Power, a rejection of the belief that non-violent protest, civil rights, liberal politics and integration would lead to real change. Others simply gave up. In her 1968 autobiography, *Coming of Age in Mississippi*, student activist Anne Moody recalled how her initial optimism gave way to a loss of faith in the ability of organizations and leaders to challenge deep-seated racism.

How global was the civil rights movement?

It's fashionable, nowadays, to see the civil rights movement as part of a broader struggle for human rights. Contemporary historians stress that in the 1950s and 1960s the world was full of oppressed groups demanding the kind of freedoms envisaged in the United Nation's lofty 1948 Declaration of Human Rights.

Take the following two examples. One, in late spring 1963, was the bus boycott in the city of Bristol, the first of its kind in Britain. The aim was to overturn the council's refusal to employ black or Asian drivers. The boycott was led by a young social worker, Paul Stephenson, the son of a West African man and a white English woman. Stephenson said he had been inspired by the actions of Rosa Parks in Montgomery, Alabama, eight years earlier. The boycott won support from leading Labour MPs, including the future prime minister, Harold Wilson. Six months later, after much debate, the council dropped the so-called "colour bar".

In February 1965, in Australia, Charles Perkins, a student at Sydney University, set out on a fact-finding mission. His aim was to highlight the plight of Australia's downtrodden Aborigine population. A promising footballer, who briefly played for the English club, Everton, Perkins was himself an Aborigine – one of the first to study at an Australian university. The bus trip he led with fellow students was similar to the "Freedom Rides" which took place in the American South in the early sixties, and, as in those, the participants suffered violent assaults (though none as violent as in Birmingham, Alabama, where Bull Connor had tipped off the local Ku Klux Klan that his police would be 15 minutes late arriving at the bus station where the ride began... allowing mobs time to pummel the riders).

The actions of Stephenson and Perkins show how global the civil rights movement became, at a time when indigenous Australians, Asians, Africans, Indians, West Indians and blacks in Europe were demanding equality or gaining their independence. And while the American movement inspired protest elsewhere, American activists in turn borrowed strategies from abroad, notably the non-violent civil disobedience, or *satyagraha*, promoted by Indian nationalist leader Mahatma Gandhi. As they borrowed tactics, activists connected their struggles across borders. Some self-identified as being part of a "coloured world" or as members of the "darker races".

The decreasing cost of international travel by the 1960s meant that people, and not just news, travelled more easily. Students on exchange programmes and middle-class activists were regular visitors to the United States, and brought ideas of protest back to their home countries. In turn American leaders such as King and Malcolm X travelled widely promoting their ideas about inequality and freedom; both visited Britain in the mid sixties. Their message, as the African American intellectual and civil rights leader, W.E. B. Du Bois, once put it, was that the "colour line belts the world".

The Cold War both helped and hindered their efforts. It helped by adding to the pressure Washington felt to sort out America's social problems. Policymakers were acutely conscious, as Kennedy's Secretary of State Dean Rusk put it, that segregation was "the biggest single burden that we carry on our backs in foreign relations". There were plenty of reminders of this. In 1963, for instance, President Kennedy was challenged by the Organization of African Unity, which protested about the violence meted out against "our own kith and kin" in Birmingham, Alabama. Concerned about the reputation of the United States and the growing influence of the Soviet Union (which was always quick to publicize instances of American racism), Kennedy quickly introduced the legislation that became the Civil Rights Act of 1964. It was a wise decision. And it worked. African leaders praised the president for his intervention.

If the Cold War emboldened African American civil rights activists, however, it also constrained them. Taking advantage of anti-communist scare-mongering and the purges led by Senator Joseph McCarthy in the 1950s, Southern politicians were quick to smear civil rights groups as communist. As a result, some black activists, notably leaders of the National Association for the Advancement of Colored People (the main black protest organization of the day), made a point of publicly condemning communism. They had little choice. But in doing so they lost political allies who had fought for black workers' rights during the Depression, and against colonialism during the war years.

Some black activists on the left, though, such as W. E. B. Du Bois and his second wife, the writer and activist Shirley Graham Du Bois, defied the anti-communist pressure and tried to create an international progressive movement. But in an era of anti-communist zeal, the Du Boises found themselves marginalized, and moved to Ghana. That they ended up in a newly independent nation is yet another reminder that the civil rights movement occurred in the wider context of decolonisation struggles sweeping across Asia and Africa.

These struggles, unlike the Cold War, were entirely beneficial to the civil rights movement. When asked why they decided to protest, the first student activists in the US often spoke of the inspiration of African nationalism. Or, as the great civil rights era novelist James Baldwin put it in *The New York Times*: "All of Africa will be free before we get a lousy cup of coffee." In 1960 alone, the so-called "Year of Africa", 17 African nations gained independence.

For many, the African American struggle became part of a broader struggle of *The Wretched of the Earth*, to quote the title of an influential 1961 study of colonialism and violence by Frantz Fanon, a Martiniquan psychiatrist. Events such as the Mau Mau uprising in British Kenya in the 1950s, or the massacre of demonstrators in Sharpeville in South Africa in 1960, provided shared experience of violent repression.

Pan-African ideas about racial unity helped forge a closer bond between black activists in Africa and black activists in the US. In *American Africans in Ghana* (2006), historian Kevin Gaines shows how Kwame Nkrumah, the first president of Ghana and an ardent Pan-Africanist, urged African Americans to move to Ghana and use their skills to help build up the new country. Thousands of black Americans joined the Du Boises in their journey to West Africa, including the writer, dancer and educator Maya Angelou, the novelist Richard Wright, and black nationalist leader Malcolm X.

The connections between the civil rights movement in America and other, similar movements around the world were greatly helped by the presence of the United Nations (UN) in New York. Founded in the wake of the Second World War to replace the beleaguered League of Nations, the UN invited many politicians from newly independent countries to visit it, among them Jawaharlal Nehru from India and Ahmed Sukarno from Indonesia. In 1960, Cuban Prime Minister Fidel Castro used his visit to the UN as an opportunity to stay in Harlem and meet black leftists and nationalists, including Malcolm X – who saw Castro as a heroic figure committed to ending racism and prejudice in post-revolutionary Cuba.

What were the key events?

Early chroniclers of the civil rights movement refer to a "Montgomery to Selma" decade of high profile, set-piece demonstrations in the American South. Following the famous bus boycott in Montgomery, Alabama, of 1955, these key demonstrations included the student sit-ins of 1960 (where students "sat-in" at all white cafes until they were served), the Freedom Rides of 1961 (where teams of black and white volunteers rode buses through the South), and the major city-wide demonstrations, involving Martin Luther King, in Birmingham in 1963 and Selma in 1965. These demonstrations dominated headlines, were associated with national civil rights organizations, and won far-reaching legislation – the Civil Rights Act of 1964 and the Voting Rights Act of 1965.

By the 1980s, though, civil rights historians were acknowledging that smaller scale, local movements had also played their part. Each community had its own story to tell, stories that did not necessarily fit with – and sometimes ran counter to – the Montgomery to Selma narrative. In some parts of Mississippi, as John Dittmer notes in *Local People* – his 1995 study of the Magnolia state (so-called after its beautiful Magnolia trees) – black soldiers demanded the right to vote on their return after World War Two, while, in Tupelo, in the same state, marches didn't even *start* until the 1970s, as historian Akinyele Umoja notes in *We*

Will Shoot Back (2014).

Each of the nationally famous city campaigns grew out of local activism. Take Montgomery. A well-established Women's Political Council organized the bus boycott, and Rosa Parks was an experienced campaigner against sexual assault. The boycott, "often heralded as the opening scene of the civil rights movement, was in many ways the last act in a decades-long struggle to protect black women... from sexualized violence and rape", writes Danielle McGuire in her 2010 study of black women's activism, *At the Dark End of the Street*.

And while Montgomery, as we have seen, occupies a central place in the mythology of civil rights, it did not actually trigger the movement. Although King formed the Southern Christian Leadership Conference (SCLC) a year later to encourage protest, there were no copycat bus boycotts elsewhere. Rather, it was the 1960 sit-in protest in Greensboro, North Carolina, that marks the start of the mass phase of the civil rights movement. Copycat sit-ins, according to a leading black newspaper, the *Chicago Defender*, "ripped through Dixie with the speed of a rocket and the contagion of the old plague". By the following summer, more than 70,000 people had been involved in some sort of direct-action protest, including wade-ins on beaches, pray-ins at churches, and piss-ins in toilets. Hundreds, perhaps thousands, were assaulted and arrested.

The sit-in movement led to the creation of the

Student Nonviolent Coordinating Committee (SNCC), which sponsored student protest across the South. Recognizing that the sit-ins had only been successful in college towns, the students began targeting the most segregated parts of the rural Deep South and inner cities. Their method was to live with, learn from, and support local people. The SNCC's Freedom Summer voter registration project in 1964 saw more than 1,000 student volunteers travel to Mississippi; two students, and a local activist, were murdered on arrival; hundreds of people were arrested. In the end, black Mississippians mostly remained disenfranchised, but Freedom Summer leaders made their voices heard at the Democrat Party national convention in Atlantic City later in the year. Their protests helped put pressure on the federal government to pass the Voting Rights Act of 1965.

The sit-ins galvanized other types of protest, too. The Congress on Racial Equality, a pacifist civil rights group founded during World War Two, decided to test a 1960 Supreme Court decision ruling that travel across states should not be segregated (even between states which required segregation for transport that started and finished within the state). An interracial group – the so-called Freedom Riders – left Washington DC in May 1961 on a Greyhound bus, heading for New Orleans. The riders never made it to New Orleans. They suffered beatings, a bombing, and arrest. Some never fully recovered.

Martin Luther King's organization, the

Southern Christian Leadership Conference, initially achieved little. Five years after its founding, in 1961, it led an ill-fated protest in Albany, Georgia, that fizzled out in the face of canny policing. But in 1963 it joined what turned out to be the most influential protest of all – in Birmingham. Early in the campaign, writing from jail, King bemoaned the reluctance of white moderates to support the movement. But thanks to Bull Connor's brutal policing, and the death of four young girls at church after a bomb explosion, public opinion began to turn. One poll in 1963 showed that 42% of Americans thought race was the nation's most pressing problem (up from just 4% in a similar 1962 poll). Within a year, Congress had passed the Civil Rights Act, which prohibited segregation.

Birmingham also prompted demonstrations elsewhere – nearly 1,000 across the South in the following year, more than in any previous 12-month period. There were also more recorded school boycotts in 1964 across the North and West than in all previous years combined.

The SCLC's protest in Selma, Alabama, in 1965 followed a similar pattern to Birmingham. Joining a local voter registration drive, King spearheaded a mass campaign that provoked violence, attracted national attention, and forced the president – now Lyndon B. Johnson – to introduce legislation. The Voting Rights Act was passed later in the same year, and King, keeping up the pressure, followed this with a mass campaign for fair housing and jobs in

Chicago, before planning a Poor People's campaign in Washington DC in 1968.

He was assassinated before the Poor People's campaign got under way. His death led to the single biggest night of racial violence in the 20th century. By this stage, though, the most prominent protest events were no longer non-violent confrontations in the South, but Black Power demonstrations in the North and West.

Where did the main protests happen?

On June 23, 1963, more than 100,000 people joined a March for Freedom, in Detroit, Michigan.

SIT-INS

On Monday morning, February 1st 1960, in Greensboro, North Carolina, four black men from the North Carolina Agricultural and Technical College bought toiletries and school supplies at the downtown Woolworths.

They kept their receipts and moved to the lunch counter. When they were refused service, one of the students, Ezell Blair, explained to the cashier, politely, that they had just been served at a different counter.

When the manager asked them to leave, they refused, and "sat-in" for the rest of the day. The following day, some 25 students joined them. The day after that, black students occupied virtually all the seats. On Saturday, dozens of young

It was the first of a series of mass rallies and boycotts to convulse the motor city that summer, as protesters challenged police brutality. The following February, nearly half a million students in New York stayed at home to demand the integration of the city's schools in what was probably the single largest civil rights demonstration in American history.

These two examples illustrate a simple point. The civil rights movement was not, as is often imagined, confined to the South. It was nationwide.

Protest was nationwide because racial oppression was nationwide. There had been slavery in the North and South, even though it lasted longer – and the vast majority of slaves lived – in the South. After emancipation, there had been anti-black violence, segregation, and attempts to

white men tried to block the protesters, but members of the A&T football team formed a "flying wedge" to allow them through. Shortly afterwards, Woolworths closed after a bomb scare.

When it still refused to end segregation, students began a boycott of all stores in the city with segregated lunch counters. Overall, sales at these counters dropped by about a third. On July 25, the manager of Woolworths ordered three black employees to eat at the lunch counter. By this time, students were challenging segregation across the South.

When the Greensboro Woolworths closed in 1993, the Smithsonian Museum of National History acquired a portion of the lunch counter.

In 2010, in a ceremony to mark the 50th anniversary of the sit-in, the Smithsonian director praised "The Greensboro Four" as a reminder that ordinary people can accomplish extraordinary things.

restrict black voting in both North and South. Indeed, at the start of the 20th century, a black American was at least as likely to be lynched outside the South, such was the level of anti-black violence (though there were vastly more lynchings in the South, because of the higher number of black residents there).

Local protests, North and South, were connected through family networks, especially after the Great Migration of the 1930s. By the time of the civil rights movement, 40% of black Americans lived in northern and western states (compared to just 10% in 1900). They were connected to black Southerners through institutions such as the church, and protest organizations such as the NAACP. Above all, they were connected through the fast-growing black news media. By mid century, there were at least 150 black newspapers, more than half of which circulated across state lines, passing on information about black life, politics and protest.

Protest often took different forms in northern cities, however. During the first half of the 20th century, northern activists publicly challenged white supremacy in a way that was impossible for their Southern counterparts. A growing black population, and the opportunities provided by World War Two, led to an upsurge in protest against racially restrictive housing covenants, white-only employment in industry, the underfunding of black schools, and the segregation of public facilities.

In many cases, protests in the north and west

against legal segregation and exclusion were successful – a generation before the heyday of the civil rights movement in the South. A succession of northern and then western cities and states passed civil rights ordinances in the decade after World War Two. In other words, by the late 1950s Jim Crow segregation and disfranchisement had become a distinctly southern phenomenon – and, as a result, more vulnerable.

Protest continued in the north and west during the 1960s. With legal segregation already struck down, activists concentrated on gaining equality in lived experience. "I have a dream," Martin Luther King told the Detroit Freedom March, that one day local people "will be able to buy a house... anywhere that their money will carry them and they will be able to get a job." In cities across the northern and western states, black children stayed out of school, black workers occupied construction sites and black residents marched against landlords.

In the battle for rights in practice, gains were few, and token at best. Less than a year after the Detroit march, some 700 activists from 100 cities met together at a Northern Grassroots Conference. The headline speaker was Malcolm X, by this time the most prominent Black Nationalist spokesman in the country. The conference called for black unity and for confrontation with the government, however liberal it might seem. Such political action set the scene for Black Power later in the decade.

As the movement developed in the South, too,

activists discovered that poverty and underfunded education, coupled with white economic control and arbitrary law enforcement, were structural barriers to equality that were at least as important as segregation. Thus the student movement that started in 1960 with sit-ins in cafes near Southern campuses developed into a movement that sent volunteers into the rural Deep South to confront poverty – volunteers, who in some cases, stayed for the rest of their lives.

What was Black Power?

The phrase "Black Power" first became a rallying cry in the summer of 1966. On June 5, James Meredith set out from Memphis, Tennessee in the direction of Jackson, Mississippi. Four years earlier, Meredith had been the first black student to try to get into the University of Mississippi – the resulting violence on campus led to two deaths. Now he sought to walk through the Deep South to challenge "the overriding fear that dominates the day-to-day life of the Negro in the United States". The next day, 28 miles into Mississippi, he was shot.

Civil rights leaders decided to complete what had become known as the "march against fear". On the evening of June 16, Stokeley Carmichael, the leader of the student movement, addressed a crowd, shouting: "We been saying freedom for six years and we ain't got nothin'. What we gonna start

Burning buildings during the Watts riots in 1965

saying now is Black Power!" Some shouted back: "Black Power!" Black Power became the dominant slogan of the next few years. "This is a new day," the *Chicago Defender* observed soon afterwards. "The doctrine of passive resistance as preached by Dr. King is ebbing." Now there is a "determination to meet fire with fire". That August, in Watts in Los Angeles, black residents fought against the police. During five days of violence, 34 people were killed and some 1,000 buildings were damaged or destroyed.

For many years, historians pointed to the Meredith March and the Watts riot as a clear-cut watershed between the Civil Rights movement (1954-65) and the Black Power era (1966 onwards). At first, Black Power was negatively associated with riots in northern and western cities, the fracturing of the civil rights alliance, anti-white rhetoric, and the rise of a white backlash. Timothy Tyson, biographer of the popular, Southern, armed civil rights leader Robert F. Williams, rightly pointed out in 1998 that, for historians, "Black Power still represents a tragic departure from the civil rights dream".

In fact, as Tyson also pointed out, the ideas associated with Black Power – self-defence, black unity, and a rejection of the liberal promise of reform – had a long history. Starting with insurrections on slave ships, Africans in America had fought "fire with fire" from the outset. In the 1920s, Marcus Garvey's "Back to Africa" message of black unity clearly resonated widely – his was probably the largest black protest organization in the 20th century. When W.E.B. Du Bois met black soldiers at the end of World War One – a war, as he pointed out, intended "to make the world safe for democracy" – he found little confidence in liberal promises. There are "at least 25 in every hundred... filled to the boiling point with hatred for the white Americans never before dreamed of".

So rather than Black Power taking a deviant and damaging turn from the usual pattern, it was, perhaps, the non-violent, pro-integration, Southern civil rights movement that was out of step with many of the traditions of black protest.

Moreover, the division between Black Power and the civil rights movement is nothing like as sharp as is often imagined. As Peniel Joseph, a leading historian of Black Power studies, argued in 2006, "civil rights and Black Power, while occupying distinct branches, share roots in the same historical family tree". At the start of the Montgomery bus boycott, for example, Rosa Parks and Martin Luther King kept guns in their homes for self-protection. Malcolm X was often highly critical of Martin Luther King, calling him "a chump not a champ", but, at the local level, activists tended to admire both men.

Black Power, then, was nothing new. Or as one civil rights leader, Roy Innis, explained in 1966: "Carmichael just gave a name to what a lot of people were already thinking." Indeed Carmichael's commitment to black politics and self-defence had developed during his time working with, and learning from, local people in the rural South. In northern and western cities – where activists had already won civil rights but racial inequality remained acute – there were protests against the limits of liberalism even during the heyday of the Southern civil rights movement. In a famous speech in Detroit in 1963, which he called "Message to the Grassroots", Malcolm X called the peaceful March on Washington in August 1963 "a sellout" and a "circus, a performance that beat anything Hollywood could ever do", when white leaders "acted like they really loved Negroes". Or, as one student activist put it, "the white liberal has generally turned out to be more white than liberal whenever blacks assert themselves".

In practice, the rise of Black Power did not affect the way protests were organised or carried out. Demonstrators who chanted Black Power, after all, were calling for the same things (such as jobs and decent housing), and using the same tactics (marches and boycotts), as they had before Carmichael coined the slogan. The main changes were at the national level. Two of the major civil rights organizations, Martin Luther King's SNCC, and the Congress of Racial Equality (CORE), rejected non-violence and become black-only organizations, with King beginning to speak out against American capitalism, militarism and involvement in Vietnam.

The mainstream media portrayed Black Power as driven by anger and despair, but it was much more rational and purposeful than it was made to seem. One of its offshoots, the Black Panther Party, for example – based in California and best known for its leather uniforms, revolutionary rhetoric, and very public display of guns – had a policy platform that included calls for full employment, decent housing, and an end to police harassment. Its members ran breakfast programmes for black schoolchildren.

Black Power was popular, too. Polls suggested that a majority of black Americans supported it, and some 10,000 delegates attended a Black Power-backed assembly in 1972. It seemed in tune, moreover, with what was going on abroad, its advocates inspired by the examples of postcolonial independence in Africa, the Caribbean and South Asia.

Black Power protest had another merit in the eyes of its proponents: it worked, forcing politicians to act – albeit out of fear rather than sympathy. Time and again city governments responded to riots by channelling funds into deprived areas. At the national level President Nixon approved a proposal – called the Philadelphia Plan following protests in the so-called "city of brotherly love" – for federal contractors to include specific goals for hiring black workers and specific timetables for action.

The assassination of King on April 4, 1968, seemed to confirm the ascendancy of Black Power. After his death, violence broke out in more than 100 cities. "The philosophy of non-violence died with Dr. King, the last prince of non-violence," declared one prominent activist. But King's murder, and its aftermath, also led to commitments from municipal governments to address inequalities. And Congress quickly passed legislation – previously tied up in debates – that banned racial discrimination in the sale, renting and financing of houses. The Fair Housing Act was signed into law one week after King's murder, the final major piece of civil rights legislation of the civil rights era.

What was the role of women?

In January 1964, a group of women civil rights activists staged a sit-in in the Southern city of Atlanta – not against racism in a segregated café, but against sexism in the offices of the main student protest organization (The Student Nonviolent Co-ordinating Committee). One of the women waved a placard "NO MORE WORK til Justice Comes to Atlanta office". It was a light-hearted protest, and warmly received as such. One of the women recalled later that the placard waving was "tongue in cheek". But the jocular protest was also intended to raise a serious point. Later that year, at a retreat in Mississippi, male staff members of the student organization were given copies of an anonymous memo that warned about sexism in wider society:

> Assumptions of male superiority are as widespread and deep rooted and every much as crippling to the woman as the assumptions of white supremacy are to the Negro.

The memo noted that even in civil rights work "women who are competent, qualified, and experienced, are automatically assigned to the 'female' kinds of jobs such as typing, desk work [and] cooking".

It was a timely memo. Most civil rights

organizations at this stage offered women, at best, a token role. The initial programme for the March on Washington in 1963 did not include any women speakers at all. When Dorothy Height, president of the National Council of Negro Women, complained that women were excluded, the (male) organizers said they were already represented, because the male speakers led organizations which had women members. Martin Luther King's Southern Christian Leadership Conference, meanwhile, had no women among its senior leadership. Ella Baker, so important to the Conference's early activities in her role as executive secretary, had left. "She always felt persecuted as a woman," Coretta Scott King, Martin's wife, observed, "and I cannot say that she was not justified." Even one of King's closest and most admiring colleagues, Bernard Lee, admitted: "Martin... was absolutely a male chauvinist."

Thus black women found themselves fighting on two fronts – against racism and against sexism, not just in society in general but within the ranks of their own movement. Indeed some far-sighted women activists began to join forces with white feminists. After her rebuff by the organizers of the March on Washington, Dorothy Height set up her own "Wednesdays in Mississippi", where black and white middle-class women met together to discuss ways to build coalitions against white supremacist violence. While Ella Baker was the Secretary of the Southern Christian Leadership Conference, she told its president, Martin Luther King, that she disapproved of his charismatic style of leadership. Why did he allow such hero worship, she asked. He replied that it was what the people wanted. "Strong people don't need strong leaders," she said, and accused him directly of being pampered and aloof. Unsurprisingly, she left his organization soon afterwards.

Unlike white feminists, though, black women activists were not seeking more power relative to their menfolk. As Mississippi activist Fannie Lou Hamer put it: "I got a black husband, six feet three, 240 pounds... that I don't want to be liberated from." Black men, she and many others believed, were not the main cause of black women's oppression – under Jim Crow they had suffered the humiliation of lower wages, second-class status, and being unable to protect their families. Thus in the same year that Dorothy Height challenged the March on Washington organizers to include women, she was also arguing that one important way to improve the lives of black women was to improve job opportunities and wages for black *men*.

In the black student organizations, women found more opportunities to take a lead. One of the largest student sit-in protests, at Nashville, Tennessee was led by a female student, Diane Nash. Born in Chicago, and educated at Howard University in Washington, she helped to restart the Freedom Rides in 1961. A year later, as a strong believer in "jail not bail", she accepted a prison sentence in Mississippi rather than pay a fine – despite being pregnant (fearing negative publicity, the judge suspended her sentence). Nash would later work for King, who described her as the "driving spirit in the non-violent assault on segregation at lunch counters".

In their pursuit of civil rights, male and female black leaders tended to operate differently and to face different problems. Middle-class black women like Dorothy Height looked for opportunities to forge interracial alliances much more energetically than middle-class black men. They also did much of the crucial, day-to-day work which made protests possible. Within church-based organizations, as one historian put it, "black men led but black women organized".

Black women, meanwhile, faced the constant threat of sexual violence. In 1944, a black mother in Alabama, Recy Taylor, returning from church, was gang-raped by six white men. The local branch of the National Association for the Advancement of Colored People, the main protest organization at the time, sent in a female investigator. She and other black women sought justice for Taylor but the white rapists, borrowing the old "black women are lascivious" stereotype, argued that Taylor was a prostitute and a willing participant. The men were never found guilty. The name of the investigator was Rosa Parks.

The first historians of the movement were pre-dominantly men, who in turn portrayed the movement as a predominantly male affair. By the 1980s, however, a new wave of scholars, most of them women, were exploring in much more detail the role of women activists – and in particular the overlapping issues of race, gender and class.

One consequence of this was to highlight how acutely, during the civil rights era, black men felt their masculinity undermined by prejudice. Male activists coined the phrase "I AM A MAN", and held up placards with the same, simple message. The California-based Black Panthers were associated with ultra-masculine, militaristic clothing and language. The Panthers' display harkened back to the aggressive displays of black masculinity in previous generations, as when the black nationalist Marcus Garvey led parades of black men in uniform, and women dressed in white.

For all the efforts of revisionist historians, the civil rights movement was, and still is, widely seen as largely male-dominated. In 2011, the Association of Black Women Historians accused the makers of the award-winning film, *The Help*, of trivialising the experiences of black women domestics. In other recent films, men also take centre stage. The director of *Selma* (2015), Ava Duverney, admitted that there were not enough black women in the film. But she explained to critics that the storyline had not initially included black women *at all* – she had only agreed to direct the movie if this was changed.

How important was popular culture?

The singer Nina Simone reckoned it was two cases of racist violence in 1963 which "suddenly" made her realise "what it was to be black in America". In June, the assassination of Mississippi civil rights activist Medgar Evers "was the match that lit the fuse". Three months later, four young black girls were killed during the bombing of a Black Baptist Church in Birmingham, Alabama. In her frustration, Simone wanted to get a gun. But when she calmed down she realized that "I knew nothing about killing and I did know about music". She sat at her piano and words "erupted out of me quicker that I could write it down". Sixty minutes later, Simone produced the sheet music for "Mississippi Goddam", that told of "children sitting in jail" and the fear that "every day's gonna be my last".

Just as Simone reached for a piano rather than a gun, popular culture became a weapon for civil rights activists. It also became a battleground of the civil rights movement, where black artists competed for recognition.

Jim Crow, by enforcing segregation, did much to boost black popular culture and sport, from the rise of black baseball leagues, to the growing popularity of juke joints (bars with music) and black reading clubs. The segregation of popular culture, though, was not as firm as the segregation of schools and buses.

In 1910, for example, the black heavyweight boxer, Jack Johnson, retained his world boxing title against the former champion Jim Jeffries – the so-called "Great White Hope" who had come out of retirement to reclaim his crown. A controversial, larger than life celebrity who flaunted his relationships with white women, Johnson was wildly popular for his ability not just to beat white challengers, but to taunt and crush them. "O My Lord what a feeling," exulted one black poet, "when Jack Johnson turned Jim Jeffries's snow white face to the ceiling." A popular breakfast order was to ask for coffee as strong and black as Johnson, and for scrambled eggs beat up like Jeffries.

Less controversial, but even more poignant in the fight against white supremacy, sprinter Jesse Owens made history at the summer Olympics in Berlin in 1936 when he won four gold medals right under the gaze of Adolf Hitler.

At times black cultural expression provoked a vicious backlash – defenders of white supremacy knew what was at stake. The night Jack Johnson first won the heavyweight title witnessed the worst anti-black violence for a generation. Sometimes, though, black culture prompted admiration. What is now known as the Harlem Renaissance took advantage of white support. The rich outpouring of black music, dance, writing, and art after World War One in Harlem was facilitated by white patrons – patrons who were attracted to what they saw as

Jesse Owens after he won the Long Jump at the 1936 Olympics in Berlin - in front of Adolf Hitler

authentic – some said primitive – culture at a moment when white Western culture seemed to have been corrupted by consumption and war.

By mid century, popular culture had become an arena where racial boundaries were constantly tested. Crucially, the segregation line was crossed time and again – thereby subtly undermining segregation in other areas of American life. Jackie Robinson led the way in baseball when he signed for the Brooklyn Dodgers in 1947, and was named rookie of the year. In music, white-owned radio stations began to play cross-over artists like Simone. There was a practical financial incentive behind this rather than interracial goodwill: companies could target both black and white consumers in an age when the purchasing power of both whites and blacks was growing fast. Indeed at

Robinson's first home match black fans outnumbered white ones.

In the cases of both sport and music, commercial imperatives helped wear down prejudice.

And during the 1960s, even Hollywood began to challenge the colour line. Notoriously, the film studios had been conservative on race – if they cast black actors at all, it was invariably as racial stereotypes. The 1943 sci-fi horror *Captive Wild Woman* was a case in point: the sci-fi part was the ambition of a mad scientist to transform an animal into a human; the horror was that it was a gorilla turning into an attractive African American woman, who regressed to an ape in a fight with her love rival. Quite a contrast with the 1967 film *Guess Who's Coming Home for Dinner,* where a young woman brings home her remarkably well qualified, handsome – and black – fiancé (played by Sydney Poitier) to meet her supposedly liberal, and shocked, parents (played by Spencer Tracey and Katherine Hepburn). Two weeks after the final scene of the film was shot, the Supreme Court ruled in favour of interracial marriage – before the ruling, this was still banned in 17 states.

As civil rights protest gained momentum in the 1950s and 1960s, a relatively small yet highly influential number of black artists began to lend their support to the cause. Artists such as the actor and singer Paul Robeson, the comedian Dick Gregory and the South African singer Miriam Makeba (who joined together anti-apartheid and

American civil rights protest) performed fundraising concerts for activists. Such politically committed artists, though, were in the minority. Most avoided controversy in order to maintain their cross-over appeal. The highly successful black-owned Motown Record Company, whose stars included The Temptations and The Supremes, churned out catchy love songs rather than political anthems. It was much the same in sport, when some, but only some, high profile athletes spoke in support of the movement. The baseball star Jackie Robinson was careful to avoid causing trouble during his professional career, but following his retirement in 1957 he made contact with King, later attending the March on Washington.

The breaking of popular cultural barriers foreshadowed the challenge to segregation in society. Liberal whites, especially college students, often supported the goals of the movement. Yet the fall of segregation within popular culture also galvanised defenders of segregation who lumped together black protest, popular music and free love as a dire, multiple threat to ordered society. During a concert in Birmingham Alabama in 1956, a group of white supremacists tried to kidnap the celebrated black singer and television personality, Nat King Cole – notwithstanding the fact, as Cole pointed out later, that he had never joined a civil rights protest or organisation.

The rise of black power in the late 1960s was also represented in popular culture. The rallying cry of "black is beautiful" found expression in the fashion world through the sudden popularity of the West African Dashiki and natural "Afro" hairstyles. Musicians followed suit, with songs like Simone's popular "To Be Young, Gifted and Black", and the 'King of Soul' James Brown's "Sing It loud, I'm Black and I'm Proud", both released in 1969. Other artists influenced by black power included Marvin Gaye, whose 1971 song "What's Going On?", the first overtly political Motown hit, criticised the Vietnam war, poverty, and growing racial inequality in urban cities.

At much the same time, the so-called "black arts movement", a group of politically motivated writers and musicians, adopted an explicit Black Power agenda. Writers like Amiri Baraka (previously known as Leroi Jones) wrote of militant black nationalism and gave voice to a restless generation

MALCOLM X

Malcolm X was born Malcolm Little, in 1925 in Nebraska, to parents who were active supporters of the Jamaican black activist, Marcus Garvey. His early life was traumatic – his father was murdered, most probably by a white supremacist group; his mother had a nervous breakdown; and Malcolm ended up in foster care. At 21, he was sent to prison for burglary, where he met Elijah Muhammad, the leader of the black nationalist religious sect, the Nation of Islam.

He dropped the surname Little, since it was inherited from a slave owner, and changed it to X, as a way of of inner city black youths. Baraka himself became a leader of Black Power politics in his home town of Newark and on the national stage.

Links between popular culture and African American life continued into the 1970s and 1980s. The rise of hip-hop and rap music among black and Latino youth in the 1980s was strongly influenced by urban poverty and inequality. Grandmaster Flash and The Furious Five's 1982 hit, *The Message*, started: "It's like a jungle sometimes; it makes me wonder how I keep from goin' under." Public Enemy's 1989 hit, *Fight The Power*, meanwhile, was a challenge to the conservative politics of the Ronald Reagan era.

Increasingly, rap's authenticity and ambiguous intent came under scrutiny, however. Scholars (notably Michael Eric Dyson and Tricia Rose) have shown how while, in its origins, rap music grew

driving home the fact that his real surname had been lost.

After prison Malcolm X became the leading spokesman for the Nation of Islam, and a staunch critic of the civil rights movement. He labelled the March on Washington as a "farce on Washington", mocked the goal of integration as "coffee with a cracker", called Martin Luther King an "Uncle Tom" and condemned non-violence as a "criminal philosophy". In his Message to the Grassroots speech of 1963, he warned: "A revolution is bloody. Revolution is hostile. Revolution knows no compromise... You don't do any singing; you are too busy swinging."

After breaking with the Nation of Islam in 1964, Malcolm X travelled to newly independent African nations, the Middle East and Egypt, and to Europe. He converted to Islam and founded the Organisation of Afro-American out of the black protest movement, it also endorsed patriarchy, sexism, homophobia, capitalist consumerism, and nihilism. Ultimately, though, like all music, it was there to be enjoyed – to be listened to in clubs, cars and sitting rooms, not dissected for content. Like popular culture more generally, it was designed, first and foremost, to be popular and commercial – not to make overt political statements.

How important was religion in the movement?

"As a child, I learned from the Bible to trust in God and not be afraid." So wrote Rosa Parks at the start of *Quiet Strength,* reflecting on her guiding principles. From an early age she memorized

Unity, seeking to promote connections between black nationalists around the world, and to persuade black leaders overseas to enlist the help of the UN.

Mainstream civil rights leaders accused Malcolm X, a brilliant orator, of being all words and no action (though many, including King, accepted much of his critique of white racism and admired his praise of black Americans). For a man who joined protest movements across the United States and abroad, this was an unfair criticism. In any case, words mattered, or as one black student leader put it, "Malcolm X said aloud those things which Negroes had been saying amongst themselves". After his assassination in 1965, his autobiography quickly became the most influential text for Black Power activists. ●

scripture, found hymns a comfort, and was a devout member of the African Methodist Episcopal Church – a denomination that had been a spiritual home to many protest leaders in American history. Recalling the moment she refused to move from her seat to the back of the bus in Montgomery, she said she felt "the Lord would give me the strength to endure whatever I had to face. God did away with all my fear."

Following Rosa Parks's arrest, organisers of the bus boycott called a mass meeting at a central Baptist Church. The new Baptist minister in the city, Martin Luther King, gave the opening speech. "Mrs. Parks is a fine Christian person," King reminded the 5,000 strong crowd, "and we are a Christian people... we must keep God in the forefront. Let us be Christian in all our actions."

God was on the side of justice, he went on. "If we are wrong, God Almighty is wrong." They could be confident of victory, because God warned the unjust "I will break the backbone of your power". Following the boycott, King created his organization, the Southern Christian Leadership Conference, to stage mass civil rights demonstrations, while his later, famous "Dream" speech in Washington drew strongly on biblical imagery and form.

As the examples of Rosa Parks and King make clear, faith mattered. Many activists prayed, sang and called out to God for strength and deliverance. Religious institutions mattered, too. Churches provided a safe haven for black communities, a place for leaders to develop, and from which they could organise, protest campaigns. And theology mattered, helping instil a confidence that a loving God was on "our side" and that, crucially, an avenging God would bring judgement on segregation. As Albert Raboteau put it, in his *History of African American Religion* in 1999, the civil rights movement became "a religious crusade".

Early historians of the civil rights movement, while noting the prominence of churchmen within it, paid too little attention to this religious dimension. But it had been crucial from the outset. Opponents of slavery pointed to God's deliverance of the people of Israel in the Bible. Harriet Tubman's daring in rescuing slaves earned her the nickname "Moses". After emancipation there was a mass religious revival, as former slaves joined all-black Methodist and Baptist denominations.

Not all their dependants felt the same fervour. Following the rise of Jim Crow, many civil rights leaders questioned the nature, and even existence, of God. Although the devout Christian Ida Wells felt God had called her to campaign against lynching, other leaders asked how a loving God could allow lynching in the first place – and why the white church seemed reluctant to challenge white supremacy. Some churches, faced with this dilemma, turned their attention to a more social gospel of support for those in poverty.

One way or another, though, churches played a

crucial role throughout the civil rights era. When the movement was at its height, the black Baptist and Methodist denominations had more than seven million members and were by far the largest all-black institutions in the country. Historians of local protest movements have found that, as often as not, a clergyman or a churchwoman led local campaigns in the South, while the sociologist Aldon Morris, who wrote a comprehensive history of the *Origins of the Civil Rights Movement* (1974), concludes that the black church was its "institutional center".

But it is going too far to say that the movement was predominantly church-based or Christian. Many black clergymen, perhaps a majority, did not even open up their churches to civil rights organizations. King was part of a breakaway group of clergy from the main National Baptist Convention, which did not endorse direct action protest. Instead he and his followers formed the much smaller Progressive Baptist Convention, which did.

Moreover, many of the key protest groups of the civil rights era were *not* church-based; they were formed outside it, even though they often used churches and church halls for their meetings and worked with church leaders. For example, the Freedom Riders had Quaker roots and started their journey with silent reflection, rather than spoken prayer. Secular groups such as veterans' associations, unions, housewives' leagues and women's clubs also played vital roles – though their members, of course, were often church members, too.

In the Black Power era, the relationship between activists and the church became more difficult. There was, to quote black religious scholars Cornell West and Eddie Glaude, "a complex relationship between the religious dimensions of the Civil Rights Movement and the Black Power phase" of protest. Malcolm X, a member of the Nation of Islam before converting to Sunni Islam, dismissed Christianity as "the white man's religion... all it's done for black men is help keep them slaves". But in later life he was willing to set aside religious differences with black nationalist Christians – he called it putting his religion in his pocket – in the common fight against white supremacy. Black Power theologians, notably James Cone, explored the biblical basis for liberation, and challenged mainstream Christian portrayals of a white God. Even Martin Luther King admitted: "I'm inclined to agree with [Malcolm X] when he points out the laxities of Christianity."

The role of the white church, meanwhile, was decidedly mixed. In his call for a "beloved community" of protest, King appealed to white religious leaders to join him during campaigns. Many did, some even dying for the cause. Importantly, during the civil rights era, Southern white church denominations went on record in favour of desegregation. The failure of Southern "white supremacists to get their churches to give their cause active support... was their Achilles heel", concludes David Chappell, in *A Stone of Hope* (2005), an exploration of the power of religion during the civil rights movement.

King, though, also expressed frustration when white clergy – while opposing segregation – called on him to end his protests against segregation. And segregationists, particularly politicians, still claimed divine support for their cause. Less sympathetic to the white church than her fellow historian, David Chappell, Jane Dailey argues that scares about interracial marriage show how "deeply interwoven Christian theology was in the segregationist ideology that supported the discriminatory world of Jim Crow".

Who resisted the movement?

On January 14, 1963, George Wallace gave his inaugural speech as Governor of Alabama "in the name of the greatest people that have ever trod this earth". The speech was written by a local Ku Klux Klan organizer. "I draw the line in the dust and toss the gauntlet before the feet of tyranny," Wallace declared, referring to the federal government's involvement in Alabama's race relations. With a sentence that would become the rallying cry of southern defenders of Jim Crow, he continued: "I say segregation now, segregation tomorrow, segregation forever."

FIVE FACTS ABOUT
THE AMERICAN CIVIL RIGHTS MOVEMENT

1.

Martin Luther King is thought to have improvised his "I have a Dream" Speech. Whilst he did have notes, when he reached the stage on the Lincoln Memorial steps, he pushed them aside and produced one of the most famous and successful speeches in American History.

2.

Whilst Rosa Parks is well known to be the first lady to refuse to give up her seat on a bus, she was actually preceded by a fifteen-year-old girl called Claudette Colvin – who protested in the same manner. Claudette, too, was arrested and did jail time for her "crime", yet due to Rosa's position as secretary of the NAACP, she was thought to make a more prominent political statement.

3.

Martin Luther King's name was originally Michael, not Martin. His father, Michael King Sr. chose to change both of their names to Martin after the famous German reformer, Martin Luther in 1934.

4.
Barack Obama was born in 1961 – three years
before the American Civil Rights Act of 1964
banning discrimination against minority groups
was signed.

5.
It is thought that the Soviet Union promoted
racial friction by forging threats from the Ku
Klux Klan and having them sent to black
neighbourhoods.

Two years later, Wallace ordered state troopers to halt a civil rights march in Selma. The resulting attacks on protesters, broadcast on television, shocked the nation, including President Lyndon Johnson. "I felt a deep outrage," Johnson recalled later. Soon afterwards, Johnson urged Congress to pass a voting rights bill.

Part of the power of the civil rights movement was that it played out on television screens as a morality play: non-violent demonstrators attacked by uncouth mobs or brutal police. Little wonder that public opinion and politicians in the northern states mostly swung against southern segregationists. Little wonder, too, that historians initially paid little attention to such segregationists. They were simple, reactive, and wrong – and they lost.

In recent years, though, historians have looked with much greater care at the so-called "massive resistance" of southern segregationists and the

NANNIE BURROUGHS

Born in Virginia in 1879, the child of a domestic servant,

Nannie Burroughs attended Washington's M Street High School, one of America's first high schools for African Americans.

She wanted to become a domestic science teacher, but was denied the chance because she was black. "The pain of that disappointment," she wrote later, "inspired me to eventually establish a school that would defence of white privilege more generally. Their conclusion: white Southern segregationists were more complex, and white resistance much more sophisticated, creative, widespread and enduring, than was first assumed.

The defence of white supremacy had a long history. The Ku Klux Klan had risen in strength after the civil war and during the 1920s, long before its revival in the 1960s. But massive resistance to change in the mid-century was by no means a given. In his early career George Wallace, for example, was known as a moderate on race relations. His opposition to the Ku Klux Klan in the race for governor in 1958 earned him the support of the National Association for the Advancement of Coloured People. It was only when he lost to a staunchly segregationist opponent that he vowed: "I will never be outniggered again." He believed, in other words, that his liberal policies had cost him the election.

In many ways, the story of massive white resistance was Wallace's story writ large. Following a ruling by the Supreme Court in 1954 – the so-called *Brown* decision – to integrate schools, a segregationist stance became a political vote winner in the South. Aspiring politicians simply had to raise the spectre of white girls and black boys going to the same school, and potentially dating – interracial sex was the most sensitive of all segregation issues. The Klan took the headlines, with their hooded rallies and burning crosses, but it was White Citizens Councils, formed in response to the *Brown* decision, with members drawn from the middle and upper classes, that proved to be the greater obstacle to the civil rights movement.

White defiance of the law, however cloaked in respectability, encouraged mob violence. But, ironically, the violence in turn encouraged federal interference on behalf of the civil rights movement. When Governor Orval Faubus of Arkansas stood at the door of a white school in Little Rock Arkansas in 1957, to turn away black children, and leave them to the fury of a mob, President Dwight Eisenhower felt obliged to intervene to uphold a law which had been endorsed by the Supreme Court. No champion of black civil rights, Eisenhower sent in an Airborne Division to escort the children to school. "The harder Southern whites fought to maintain Jim Crow," noted Clive Webb, a historian of massive resistance, in 2005, "the more they seemed to accelerate its demise."

It would be wrong to stereotype all southerners as diehard segregationists. A few championed civil rights. Many were appalled by the antics of men like Wallace and Bull Connor, calling for better treatment for black southerners and negotiated, gradual change. But in a letter from jail in Birmingham, Alabama, Martin Luther King explained it was not the segregationists who were his most effective opponents, but the white moderates who advocated better race relations while telling African Americans to be patient and not to demand change.

At the height of the civil rights movement, most business and political leaders in the South made concessions to bring mass protests to an end as quickly as possible. Such leaders thought the end of segregation was preferable to downtown disturbances (and loss of trade), especially when token integration did not affect their daily lives. After all, the ending of segregation on buses and in city centre stores and parks was of little concern to those who owned their own cars, lived in the suburbs and were members of country clubs.

As with the struggle for racial equality, the famous confrontations of the 1960s did not mark the end of the defence of white privilege. Many city dwellers moved to all-white suburbs, where schools and amenities were white-only irrespective of civil rights legislation. Polls showed that while a white majority *supported* the end of segregation and was in favour of diversity in the workplace, they *opposed* laws to require integration of schools by bussing children into different neighbourhoods, or affirmative action to ensure minority participation at work or in higher education. Thus the very successes of the civil rights movement prompted a backlash by the so-called "silent majority" of voters which wanted a roll-back of civil rights legislation. In his 2006 book *The Silent Majority,* Matthew Lassiter argues that this silent majority believed that any advantages white Americans had in jobs and housing were the "outcome of meritocratic individualism rather than the unconstitutional product of structural racism".

Modern historians have looked not just at white resistance to civil rights but, more generally, at the entrenchment of white privilege. In *The Wages of Whiteness* (1991), David Roediger explores how working class white Americans accepted low wages in return for the privileged status of being white in a society with a hierarchy based on race. Thomas Sugrue, in his 1996 book, *The Origins of the Urban Crisis,* shows that the business and social policies of successive governments left a higher proportion of black Americans unemployed and, by creating inner city ghettoes with cheap housing, reinforced negative racial stereotypes. In short, the idea of whiteness was entrenched, adaptable, and powerful. Nell Irving Painter, an African American historian, predicted in *The History of White People* (2010), that "the notion of American whiteness will continue to evolve, as it has since the creation of the American republic". She meant that the white majority would continue to find ways of resisting equality, however skilfully it might appear to be doing the opposite.

How much of a difference did politicians make?

"Dr. King's dream began to be realized when President Johnson passed the Civil Rights Act. It took a president to get it done." In her campaign against Barack Obama to be the Democrats' presidential candidate in 2008, Hilary Clinton made much of experience in government. And her comment raises an important question: how much were American civil rights successes the result of grassroots pressure, and how much of far-sighted decision-making in Washington?

A decade earlier, in *Debating the Civil Rights Movement,* historians Steven Lawson and Charles Payne addressed this very question and drew very different conclusions. Lawson argued that the "federal government played an indispensable role in shaping the fortunes of the civil rights revolution". The movement would have happened without federal support, he said, but it would have "lacked the power and authority to defeat state governments".

Payne, however, a historian of the grassroots

struggle in Mississippi, questioned the notion that civil rights gains were the result of "the weight of American institutions" finally being "brought to bear" on the longstanding problem of Jim Crow. In fact, he said, there's a good case to be made that the opposite is true – that, far from being the solution, "American institutions have always played key roles in the creation and maintenance of racism". Any successes were due to activists finding a way "to manoeuvre round those institutions to alleviate some of the worst features of the system".

Ultimately, of course, it was not a case of either/ or, as both historians readily acknowledged. Grassroots pressure and federal action invariably worked together. The landmark *Brown* decision against school segregation of 1954 was a ruling by an increasingly liberal Supreme Court on five cases, brought by scores of parents who had been protesting against segregated schools for a decade. Some of those parents had lost their jobs and been run out of town for pursuing legal action. Similarly, the legislation that became the Civil Rights Act in 1964 was introduced by President Kennedy, who, though personally opposed to Jim Crow, was reacting to massive demonstrations in Birmingham, Alabama.

Taking a long view of the movement, Payne is clearly right to portray federal institutions as creators, defenders or ignorers of inequality. In the Plessy v Ferguson case of 1896, the Supreme Court endorsed segregation on public transport in New

Orleans, and by extension, supported the rise of segregation across the South. In the early 20th century, President Woodrow Wilson oversaw the segregation of government departments. With its committees mostly chaired by southern Democrats (on account of their longevity in post), Congress did not champion civil rights – and did not even pass anti-lynching legislation. Malcolm X complained in 1964 that even when the committees "let something through... usually it is so chopped up and fixed up that by the time it becomes law, it is a law that can't be enforced".

Change tended to come only in response to significant external pressure. When Franklin Roosevelt issued Executive Order 8802 in 1942, banning discrimination in the national defence industry, he did so after a threatened mass march on Washington and at a time when the wartime government needed national unity. Similarly, Kennedy acted in part because leaders of newly independent African nations had made it clear that the anti-black violence in Birmingham would cost him their support just when he most needed it in the Cold War.

Indeed, it is striking just how much pressure had to be brought to bear to force federal involvement during the civil rights campaign. Though Kennedy had run on a pro-civil rights electoral platform, as president he had said little about civil rights, and done less, before the Birmingham campaign. Even when he did act, it was more out of concern about disorder than social change. His successor, Lyndon Johnson, was genuinely committed to civil rights, and made the passage of the Civil Rights Act a priority. But in his inaugural address in 1965, he did not mention voting rights, and told Martin Luther King in private that there was no chance of pushing voting rights legislation through Congress that year. It was the bloody protests in Selma that forced his hand.

Given this long history of grassroots pressure and federal resistance, the changing outlook – however minimal – of federal officials during the mid 20th century mattered greatly. It helps explain why the civil rights movement was able to make the type of gains that it did, when it did. By the time of the 1954 Supreme Court ruling against segregated schools in the *Brown* decision, the idea of racial hierarchies had been discredited intellectually. Thus the Court was receptive to the arguments of civil rights lawyers, even though politicians were not yet willing to insist on *Brown*'s implementation. A decade later, though, Congress acted.

By this time Democrats outside the south were more responsive to the demands of black voters – now *their* voters, following the Great Migration. By the same token, for the first time southern Democrats no longer had a stranglehold over Congress. It also helped that Lyndon Johnson was a master of Washington politics and personally committed to civil rights. Thus when the protests in Birmingham and Selma and elsewhere shocked the

nation, the federal government was willing to act.

If federal action responded to grassroots pressure, though, the reverse was true, too. Protests by black workers led to the introduction in 1967 of the Philadelphia Plan, which required federal projects to hire an appropriate proportion of black workers. In turn, however, the Plan – coupled with the Civil Rights Act – gave workers new power to demand equality in the workplace. In the late 1960s and early 1970s, there were confrontations, demonstrations and instances of litigation in textile mills across the south and at construction sites in the north. Minority hiring, as a result, rose quickly in both industries. In the same way, the Voting Rights Act prompted major voting rights campaigns across the south.

In his 2002 book, *Minority Rights Revolution*, political scientist John Skrenty argues that one unexpected legacy of the civil rights movement was that, for the first time, the government began to take the initiative on extending rights *even without grassroots pressure*. The explanation lay in the federal bureaucracy. Civil rights activism forced through legislation in the 1960s, which in turn led to the expansion of government agencies that were staffed by those committed to civil rights and eager to work with advocacy groups. Thus the Civil Rights Act included other minority groups even though the movement had only called for black rights. Later in the 1960s the government extended support for bilingual education and Latino businesses even though no group had lobbied or protested on these issues.

PEYTON WALL

In December 1962, Atlanta's mayor ordered the construction of barricades on two roads in the Peyton Forest area, to the west of the city. Over the previous decade, white Atlantans had moved out of the inner city to this prosperous suburb. Much to the alarm of the home owners, African Americas were starting to head west, too, and buying homes in the white section of town.

The barricades were designed to halt the spread of black home-owning, and thus to defuse tension. They did precisely the opposite. Civil

In studying the role of government in civil rights it is important not to lose sight of the broader picture. Protest was not just about winning new rights, but about inspiring people to challenge white supremacy in everyday life, and to demand equality in the future. Victories in Washington were an important part of this, but by no means the only part.

What role did the media play?

On August 28, 1963, the activist and journalist Eslanda Robeson was in East Berlin, watching television coverage of the March on Washington with her husband, the opera singer Paul Robeson. "We could almost feel ourselves there, in person, in Washington," she wrote. Barely two weeks later,

rights activists picketed, denouncing Atlanta's "Berlin Wall". White home-owner groups celebrated, and put Christmas decorations on the barricades. Black residents bought homes to the west of the wall anyway. In February, violence followed, undercutting the city's claim to be "Too Busy To Hate" because of its economic progress, moderate politics and acceptance of token desegregation in schools and transport.

Local courts ruled the barricade illegal. Weeks later, most homes on the white side of the road were up for sale, listed with black estate agents. It was a saga by no means unique to Atlanta: many other cities had similar experiences in the 1960s and 1970s. ●

the Ku Klux Klan bombed the Sixteenth Street Baptist Church in Birmingham, Alabama, killing four young African American girls. On hearing the news, residents of Llansteffan, a small village in Wales, responded by raising money to replace the main stained-glass window that had been damaged.

That events in the United States could elicit pride in Berlin, or sympathy in Wales, illustrates the impact of the media on civil rights. And activists were acutely conscious of how media interest could be exploited, given the tendency of television, in particular, to present the demonstrations as a moral drama. By the time of the student sit-ins more than eight in every ten homes in the United States had a television – compared with barely one in ten a decade earlier. The 1962 launch of the Telstar satellite allowed TV coverage to be broadcast across the Atlantic.

The visual impact of seeing attacks on non-violent men, women, and children did much to swing public opinion behind the civil rights movement, as opinion polls showed. Some 50 million watched the brutal beatings of marchers in Selma. The fact that ABC interrupted its broadcast of the war crimes film, *Judgement at Nuremberg,* to switch to the drama in Selma was an irony not lost on commentators. Lyndon Johnson, watching live on television, recalled later: "I felt a deep outrage." (He was appalled not only by the violence but by King's control of the agenda. "I just think it's outrageous what's on TV," Johnson told one aide.

"I'm watching it here and it looks like that man is in charge of the country.") Johnson felt obliged to introduce voting rights legislation.

Civil rights activists understood the importance of media coverage and often made decisions based on the likely publicity. In Montgomery, Alabama, for instance, a young African American woman called Claudette Colvin refused to give her seat on a bus some nine months before Rosa Parks famously did the same. But because she was unmarried and pregnant, and had a reputation for being "mouthy", local leaders did not publicize her cause. Instead, they would back Rosa Parks, a respectable, church-going, married seamstress.

As the movement progressed, activists became more sophisticated in their handling of the media. Black students set up a communications department, cultivating sympathetic reporters in the national press and sending out an abundance of press releases. Martin Luther King became adept at using television, staging non-violent protests that would provoke violent reactions and thus setting up the kind of "good vs evil" battles that would win sympathy from viewers of the evening news. He also used press conferences to devastating effect. After a secret meeting with Lyndon Johnson during the Selma campaign in 1965, King announced to reporters that he had met the president, and had been assured that the president "was determined" to remove obstacles to African American voting – even though President Johnson had said no such thing publicly.

If the media was useful as a tool to change public opinion, it was also a means to spread news among African Americans. Ironically, it was Jim Crow which first gave impetus to black media, since the segregated society led to the emergence of a separate black press. The proliferation of black newspapers meant there was plenty of space for critical debates about race and equality, and news of protest from around the country and across the world could now easily be shared.

In the early 20th century, some black newspapers gained a national readership. The most famous of them, the *Chicago Defender,* had an estimated readership of half a million, and promoted the Great Migration that saw millions of African Americans move to northern cities. As protests began to gather momentum in the 1950s and 1960s the readership of these papers expanded, and the stories they carried also appeared in black-owned newspapers in London, Paris, and West Africa.

The glossy black magazines *Ebony* and *Jet*, both founded after the war, gave valuable space to black entertainers and sportsmen, as well as to civil rights leaders like King. Though neither magazine was overtly political, both supported the movement. Meanwhile, religious periodicals such as the African Methodist Episcopal Review contained lengthy reflections on protest and freedom.

The emergence of radio helped, too. By the 1940s, most black families had access to a radio, and by 1955 more than 20 radio stations in the south devoted the bulk of their air time to a black audience. Most of these stations were white owned, and their raison d'etre was music not politics. But, as Brian Ward says in *Radio and the Struggle for Civil Rights in the South* (2004), DJs could use coded language to let listeners know where a demonstration might be occurring, or on which streets police were patrolling.

On the whole, the media had a positive impact on the movement, although, as in other areas of public life, it had a tendency to over-simplify things. The intense focus on King meant that local leaders, many of them women, were often overlooked. And it was easier to portray the battle against segregation (and brutal segregationist sheriffs), than to explore more complex forms of prejudice. King, for instance, found it frustrating to be known more for his dreams of freedom than for his calls to address economic injustice. "The Martin Luther King people talk about," he told a friend, is "somebody foreign to me". Malcolm X was similarly frustrated by his media portrayal as an extremist. The first television documentary to cover him was titled "The Hate that Hate Produced".

What did the civil rights movement achieve?

In 1954, the Supreme Court ruled in *Brown vs Board of Education* that "separate educational facilities are inherently unequal". A decade later President Lyndon Johnson signed a Civil Rights Act which outlawed Jim Crow segregation, called for an end to school segregation, and prohibited discrimination in employment. The following year, 1965, Johnson signed the Voting Rights Act.

These hard-earned, stunning victories dismantled the system of southern white supremacy a century after the first promise of freedom. John Lewis, the leader of the student protest movement, who had suffered numerous beatings and periods in jail on behalf of the cause, reckoned that the Voting Rights Act was "every bit as momentous as the Emancipation Proclamation".

Maybe so, but the *Brown* decision had no timetable for ending school segregation, with the court calling only for "all deliberate speed". A decade later, barely two per cent of black children in the south went to integrated schools. The Civil Rights Act did not authorize bussing of children across neighbourhoods to integrated schools, and thus had little effect on those in black inner cities or all-white suburbs. The Civil Rights Act ruling against workplace discrimination had no enforcement power. Some sections of the Voting

Rights Act were in place for only five years.

So legislation, as critics never tired of pointing out, had its limits. Reacting to the murder of three civil rights workers in Mississippi in 1964, and the FBI's failure to bring the culprits to justice, Malcolm X scoffed: "No matter how many bills pass, our lives are not worth two cents." Five days after the passage of the Voting Rights Act, residents of Watts, Los Angeles, reacted violently to news of police brutality, protesting that segregation was increasing and unemployment rising – *despite* local civil rights legislation.

On the one hand, then, the civil rights movement forced the government to pass legislation that would have been unimaginable at the height of Jim Crow. On the other, the legislation on its own did not automatically or immediately change the lived experience of black Americans. The new rights had to be made real, and Black Power advocates in particular said the rights were not nearly enough to counter the legacy, and continuing problem, of racism.

It is important, too, to remember that the headline civil rights victories of the 1960s were only possible because of the protests and pressure of previous decades. It took a threatened march on Washington during World War Two to persuade President Roosevelt to issue Executive Order 8802, outlawing discrimination in the defence industry – the first government proclamation in favour of civil rights since the Civil War era. NAACP lawyers won Supreme Court cases that began to challenge the legal basis for Jim Crow segregation, and that ruled against the Democratic Party's white-only primary election in the South. (The primary was more important than the general election in the south, given the Democrats' almost total domination of the region at the time.) In the north and west during the 1940s and 1950s, activists won city and state ordinances against discrimination and segregation.

These early victories mattered. The changing opportunities for black workers during World War Two meant that the average income of black Americans rose faster during the 1940s than in any other decade in the century – a vital precondition for the rise of a movement with the power to boycott and fund protest.

When Democratic primaries were opened up to black voters, the impact was quickly felt. Suddenly black voters had the power to force the removal of racist police officers or hardline defenders of the status quo. Activists then pressed for further concessions with sit-ins and other protests, and took advantage of civil rights gains already achieved in the north and west.

In much the same way, the *Brown* decision, the Civil Rights Act and the Voting Rights Act enabled further change. A decade after *Brown*, following the civil rights movement and continued pressure from activists, the Supreme Court made a series of rulings that called for school integration "at once" and approved bussing of students to ensure "the greatest possible degree of actual desegregation".

After the death of Martin Luther King in 1968, Congress passed the Fair Housing Act. And after massive protests that sometimes turned violent, President Richard Nixon – previously an outspoken opponent of government action to redress racial inequality – approved the so-called Philadelphia Plan requiring contractors to include specific "goals" for the hiring of non-white workers and specific "timetables" to achieve those goals.

Politically, the results of all this were spectacular. By 1977, more than 200 cities had black mayors. In the rural south, there were almost 5,000 elected officials by 1980. Despite the progress, though, American elections remained anything but equal. A white southerner was still 16 times more likely to get elected than a black southerner, and black mayors inherited a shrinking tax base, due to white flight to the suburbs and inner city decline. Still, black representatives had a platform to defend their interests, and black mayors had the power to demand a more equitable distribution of resources and appointments.

In employment, the results were decidedly mixed. Civil rights legislation and protest enabled black workers to move into skilled and semi-skilled industry at an unprecedented rate, but they did so at just the moment that heavy industry was in decline, and when new higher-tech industries were based in the (mostly all-white) suburbs. By 2000, the average net wealth of African Americans proportional to that of white Americans was in decline, down to one fourtenth. By this time, the proportion of black families in poverty – one quarter – was the lowest on record but it was nearly three times the proportion of white families in poverty, the highest gap on record.

By keeping up the pressure through their constant demands and protests, the leaders of the civil rights movement inspired a future generation of activists to follow their example – an important point in any consideration of the movement's successes. But we need to recognize its failures, too. The major organizations often failed to address issues that were linked to racial equality but went beyond it – such as the rights and welfare of black women or the problems facing the unemployed. Nor, for the most part, did civil rights leaders challenge the structural inequalities that many felt bedevilled America: the division of cities into white and black districts and the growing proportion of black prisoners in American jails.

Did other social groups benefit?

In many ways 1968 marked the end of the civil rights era. It was the year that saw the murder of

Martin Luther King making a speech in 1964, four years before his death.

Martin Luther King, the passage of the final major piece of federal civil rights legislation, and the election of Richard Nixon to the presidency. After running with an appeal to the so-called "silent majority" of voters, Nixon acknowledged, soon after taking office, that he was not seen as "a friend by many of our black citizens". That was an understatement. During his first year as president Nixon did not appoint a single African American to his cabinet, nominated a southern segregationist to the Supreme Court, denounced bussing children across neighbourhoods in order to integrate schools, and spoke out against the renewal of the Voting Rights Act.

But 1968 did not mark the end of protest. Quite

the opposite. In many smaller Southern towns, confrontational demonstrations actually began for the first time in the 1970s. Local people drew on the examples of the civil rights movement, and, just as importantly, took advantage of 1960s civil rights and voting rights laws to challenge discrimination. Or, as one demonstrator in Mississippi put it: "We are taking up where the movement of the 1960s left off."

Activists sought to turn their new rights of the 1960s into real gains in everyday life. At the ballot box, there were spectacular successes across the south, and some major gains in employment. There were protests about issues that had not been

THE CIVIL RIGHTS AND VOTING RIGHTS ACTS

The landmark Civil Rights Act of 1963 had a troubled birth. It was held up briefly in the House of Representatives and then, much more seriously, in the Senate, where Southern Senators staged a marathon 60-day filibuster in an effort to stop its passage. (A filibuster is essentially an attempt to talk a bill down by making long speeches designed to use up all the debating time.)

The eventual act, passed in 1964, was wide-ranging. Title I made unequal application of voter registration requirements illegal; Titles II and III ruled against discrimination in public accommodations and facilities; Title IV enabled the Attorney General to file suit to enforce the desegregation of public schools; Title V expanded the powers of the Civil Rights Commission; Title VI prohibited discrimination by any agency that received public funds, and Title VII prohibited addressed by the major campaigns of the 1960s, especially the rights of black women. Black women leaders, mostly marginalized by the major civil rights and Black Power organizations, came to the fore. Johnnie Tillmon, for example, a campaigner for the rights of black mothers on welfare, confronted Martin Luther King in 1968 for ignoring her concerns when he was organising a Poor People's Campaign. Five years later, seeking "dignity, justice, full citizenship and an adequate income", Tillmon's National Welfare Rights Organisation claimed a membership of 200,000 people. Through lobbying, demonstrations and providing support to members, it helped to stem

any major employer or union from discrimination on account of color, race, religion, sex or national origin.

Though a landmark piece of legislation, the Act did not have strong enforcement powers. By contrast the Voting Rights Act, signed into law in August 1965, following the protests in Selma, contained strong enforcement provisions against parts of the country where discrimination was most stark. In such areas the Attorney General had the power to appoint federal examiners to ensure fair elections, and any local changes to voting procedures had to gain preclearance from the Attorney General. The US Department of Justice notes that the Act "has been called the single most effective piece of civil rights legislation ever passed by Congress".

In 1972, Congress amended Title VII of the 1964 Act "to correct the defects of its own legislation. The promises of equal job opportunity made in 1964 must be made realities." The Amendments gave an Equal Employment Opportunity Committee the power to sue employers and unions, and ruled that state and local government employees were also covered by the provisions of the Act.

welfare cutbacks.

The civil rights and Black Power movements inspired the black freedom struggle beyond the US, too. There were sit-ins in Cape Town as part of the campaign against apartheid in South Africa, and marches in solidarity with the March on Washington in other cities round the world. In most cases local campaigners were not actually facing Jim Crow-style segregation, but used the global popularity of the American civil rights movement to benefit their own battles against discrimination.

More broadly, the various American "rights" movements of the era – pushing for equal rights for women, or gays, or Indians, or campaigning against war – drew on the example and rhetoric of civil rights and Black Power. In the aftermath of the Stonewall Riots of 1969 in New York, for example – where people fought back against a police raid of a gay bar – crowds outside the bar shouted "Gay Power". A decade later, a team of gay and lesbian activists staged a "Freedom Ride" across New York City, drawing inspiration from civil rights protests against segregated transport in their attempts to win support for a gay civil rights bill.

Ironically, even movements that *opposed* black rights and integration drew on civil rights language. Home owners defended white suburbs by speaking of their rights of association. Some conservatives specifically cited Martin Luther King's call for an America where colour didn't matter to challenge affirmative action (the practice of actively favouring black over white candidates in job selection). In Boston, demonstrators against the bussing of children pointed to the example of King's civil disobedience to justify their own campaigns. Some even sang the anthem of the civil rights movement: "We Shall Overcome."

It was not all one-way traffic, though. The civil rights movement borrowed from other movements – the sit-ins, for example, had been used in labour protests, and King was inspired by Mahatma Gandhi's non-violent demonstrations in the Indian campaign for independence from the British Empire.

African American leaders did not always welcome a coalition of the disadvantaged. Worried that other groups were competing for inclusion under affirmative action, veteran civil rights activist Julian Bond asked: "How did the civil rights road get so crowded?" Many black feminists criticised the white feminist movement's emphasis on middle class rights. Fannie Lou Hamer, a civil rights activist from Mississippi, and a founding member of the National Organisation for Women, distanced herself from NOW's pro-choice stance and called for the empowerment of, not liberation from, black men.

If Nixon's election marked the end of the civil rights era, Ronald Reagan's election in 1980 threatened a conservative roll-back of hard-earned gains. But again, protest continued, much of it defensive. Activists sought to defend previous victories, such as affirmative action in the workplace and in university admissions. But they challenged Reagan, too. The Free South Africa Movement helped to force his administration to impose sanctions on the apartheid regime. And at the local level, diverse groups of activists addressed a wide range of issues, from seeking a minimum wage for those on welfare-to-work schemes, to demanding equal chances of promotion in the boardroom.

Many of the continuing battles for equality – as in the areas of education, housing, policing, and prisons – had a long history. But some were new. The dumping of toxic waste, for example, disproportionately affected black communities. In 1982, demonstrators in Warren County, North Carolina, marched from a local church to a landfill site, to lie down and block trucks carrying toxic soil. One reporter reckoned it "was like a flashback to the 1960s". As with the 1960s' sit-ins, the lie-downs spawned copycat protests. In 2002, more than 1,000 delegates representing community-based organizations attended a People of Color Environment Leadership Summit. The so-called environmental justice movement would challenge civil rights organizations to take note of the environment, and environmental groups such as Greenpeace, to take notice of racial inequality.

The unequal impact of environmental damage on black communities was highlighted in August, 2005, when Hurricane Katrina wreaked havoc on the levees of New Orleans. Most of the nearly

2,000 victims were elderly, trapped in the rising waters, as many white as black. But television pictures mostly showed black bodies floating in the waters, and black families crammed into the Louisiana Superdome under armed guard. The lone black Senator, Barack Obama, commented: "The poverty and the hopelessness were there long before the hurricane. All the hurricane did was to pull the curtain back for all the world to see."

What the world didn't see were the activists who sought to repair their communities, and fight for equality in debates about the future of the city – people like a former Black Panther Malik Rahim, who described his campaign to bring in student volunteers as the second "Freedom Rides".

What of the future?

"Racial Barrier Falls in Decisive Victory," said a headline in the *New York Times* on November 5th 2008. With the election of the first African American President, had the US entered a new post-racial phase in its history?

Many commentators remarked that if it had not been for the civil rights movement, Barack Obama would not have been able win the presidential election. This was Obama's own view, too. In the book he wrote ahead of his presidential campaign, *The Audacity of Hope,* he described himself as a "pure product" of the sixties, because "as the child of a mixed marriage, my life would have been impossible, my opportunities entirely foreclosed, without the social upheavals that were taking place". Reflecting on his work as a community organizer in a deprived, predominantly African American neighbourhood of Chicago in the 1980s, he said that progress "must start with completing the unfinished business of the civil rights movement – namely, enforcing non-discrimination laws in such basic areas as unemployment, housing, and education".

During the election, however, he distanced himself from former civil rights leaders, positioning himself as a black candidate who could appeal to white voters and promising to pursue policies that would help all Americans, regardless of colour. His support for affirmative action was balanced by a commitment not to diminish the opportunities for

COMBAHEE RIVER COLLECTIVE

Frustrated by American feminism's lack of attention to racial discrimination, and the civil rights and Black Power movement's lack of attention to gender discrimination, black women activists formed the National Black Feminist Organization in 1973.

The following year, a group of black feminists in Boston began to meet separately. Calling themselves the Combahee River Collective, in tribute to Harriet Tubman's Combahee River Raid to free slaves during the civil war, the Collective condemned the multiple oppressions faced by women of colour, and the difficulty of collective organising.

white students. He also subscribed to the notion that individual behaviour was very important in combating racism. In particular, he called on black men to stop using excuses to explain their absence from family households and act as responsible, *present*, black fathers.

Obama did his best to stop his campaign being dominated by race, though with mixed success. His efforts to downplay the issue weren't helped by the inflammatory sermons of the Rev. Jeremiah Wright, senior pastor at Trinity United Church of Christ in Chicago. This was the church where the Obamas had married, baptised their two daughters and which, from time to time, they still attended. Wright's denunciations of America for racism and hypocrisy received copious coverage, with one quote in particular – "God damn America" – proving a gift for the headline writers..

As the controversy threatened to derail his campaign, Obama distanced himself from Wright's remarks, and directly addressed the issue of "the racial stalemate we've been stuck in for years". In a much-praised speech in Philadelphia, he called for understanding of the suffering and resentment of both black and white communities, and for a commitment to move beyond division. Obama expressed "a conviction rooted in my faith in God and my faith in the American people – that working together we can move beyond some of our old racial wounds".

With well-crafted speeches like this, Obama went on to secure the Democratic Party nomination, and then the presidency. But on assuming office he was quick to warn against wishful thinking about America suddenly turning into a "post-racial" society. Ironically, indeed, it was often those *opposed* to civil rights legislation who used the post-racial thesis most forcefully, arguing that, with an African American in the White House, there now needed to be a "colour-blind" approach to politics and the law – and that insisted legislation must no longer take account of historic (let alone current) racism.

It was never a convincing argument, as continuing evidence of racial violence showed. In the final year of Obama's first term, a black teenager, Trayvon Martin, was murdered while walking home from a convenience store in Sanford, Florida. His murderer, George Zimmerman, a neighbourhood watch volunteer who claimed Martin was suspicious, was not even arrested initially (though he was later arrested and acquitted). Obama commented: "If I had a son he would look like Trayvon."

In Obama's second term, another black teenager, Michael Brown, was murdered, this time by a white police officer, Darren Wilson, in Ferguson, Missouri. The fact that his body lay uncovered on the street for hours after the shooting, that witnesses reported Brown raised both hands in the air, and that Wilson was not charged, sparked outraged protests. These killings were by no means isolated incidents and a new pressure group, Black Lives Matter, was formed to keep pressing for change.

The White House responded with various initiatives but, as ever, it was hard to please everyone. Cornel West, a civil rights scholar, initially supported Obama, but later criticized his lack of attention to the structural roots of racism and poverty. The political scientist Melissa Harris-Perry, on the other hand, argued that the Affordable Care Act ("Obamacare") did much to reduce the racial disparities in healthcare provision.

Whatever the truth of these arguments, it is clear that America under Obama was still a long way from the "post-racial" society anticipated by the New York Times, as indeed it still is.

That said, it has come a long way since the 1950s. In September 2016, Obama attended the opening of the first National African American

History and Culture Museum in Washington. The museum is designed to commemorate the role of African Americans in American history and traces their triumphs and tribulations from slavery to the present. Henry Louis Gates, a professor at Harvard, wrote in The New York Times:

> More than a museum, the building on the National Mall is a refutation of two and a half centuries of the misuse of history to reinforce a social order in which black people were enslaved, then systematically repressed and denied their rights when freed.

Obama himself acknowledged that the museum would "not alleviate poverty... eliminate gun violence [or] wipe away every instance of discrimination in a job interview, or a sentencing hearing, or folks trying to rent an apartment". But it was vital to remember black history because it "is central to our American story". It was "a glorious story, one that is complicated, and it is messy, and it is full of contradictions, as all great stories are". And given the troubles of the times, "it's a story that perhaps needs to be told now more than ever".

First published in 2024 by
Connell Guides
Artist House
35 Little Russell Street
London WC1A 2HH

10 9 8 7 6 5 4 3 2 1

Picture credits:
p.13 © Bettmann/ Getty Images
p.33 © The LIFE Picture Collection / Getty Images
p.45 © AFP / Stringer / Getty Images
p.73 © Bettmann/ Getty Images
p.87 © Bettmann/ Getty Images

A CIP catalogue record for this book is available from the British Library.
ISBN 978-1-911187-52-3

Design © Nathan Burton

Printed in Great Britain

www.connellguides.com